ISBN 978-1-333-99239-2
PIBN 10578171

For support please visit www.forgottenbooks.com

# 1 MONTH OF
# FREE
# READING

at

## www.ForgottenBooks.com

By purchasing this book you are eligible for one month membership to ForgottenBooks.com, giving you unlimited access to our entire collection of over 700,000 titles via our web site and mobile apps.

To claim your free month visit:

www.forgottenbooks.com/free578171

English
Français
Deutsche
Italiano
Español
Português

# www.forgottenbooks.com

**Mythology** Photography **Fiction**
Fishing Christianity **Art** Cooking
Essays Buddhism Freemasonry
Medicine **Biology** Music **Ancient**
**Egypt** Evolution Carpentry Physics
Dance Geology **Mathematics** Fitness
Shakespeare **Folklore** Yoga Marketing
**Confidence** Immortality Biographies
Poetry **Psychology** Witchcraft
Electronics Chemistry History **Law**
Accounting **Philosophy** Anthropology
Alchemy Drama Quantum Mechanics
Atheism Sexual Health **Ancient History**
**Entrepreneurship** Languages Sport
Paleontology Needlework Islam
**Metaphysics** Investment Archaeology
Parenting Statistics Criminology
**Motivational**

No. 429.

THE

# ABSURDITIES OF POPERY.

PART IV.

LONDON:

PUBLISHED BY JOHN MASON, 14, CITY-ROAD;

AND SOLD AT 66, PATERNOSTER-ROW.

London: R. Needham, Printer, 1, Belle-Sauvage-Yard, Ludgate-Hill.
429.

C. Richards, Printer, 100, St. Martin's-lane, Charing Cross.

# THE ABSURDITIES OF POPERY.

To show that Popery is unchanged, and unchangeable, we present to the reader an extract from a work published in Paris, 1836, entitled " The Life and Miracles of St. Philomene." This book is translated from the Italian, and is exceedingly curious ; and it shows that the religion of Rome is precisely the same, at this moment, as it was in the very worst days of Papal idolatry ; and that the same means are resorted to by the priesthood of these days to perpetuate ignorance and superstition, as were resorted to in the darkest ages of delusion and barbarism. The original work in the Italian language has, within a very few years, gone through fifteen editions. One of these editions has the "Imprimatur" of that execrable tribunal, the Inquisition, Dec. 12th, 1833. Another of them is addressed to the Bishops, Archbishops, and Princes of the Church ; and the French translation is recommended "to the faithful" by the exhortation of the Bishop of Stratsburg. To a stranger, unacquainted with the absurdities and abominations of Popery, the contents of this volume will appear unaccountable. Such a mass of blasphemy, ignorance, and childishness was hardly ever put together in one small book. The writer details the finding of the body of the saint after this wise :—

" The body of Philomene was found May 25th, during the trenchings which are made yearly at Rome, in the

429.          A 2

4

places consecrated for the burial of the martyrs. During these preparations, the workmen struck against a tombstone of burnt, earth, and on raising the stone, the remains of the saint appeared ; and those who were present, and among them were men of cultivated minds, were astonished at perceiving the sacred particles transformed into various precious and brilliant substances, presenting the brightness and colour of gold, silver, diamonds, rubies, emeralds, and other precious stones." The following are the ways in which the revelation was made of the saintship of these newly-discovered bones : the first revelation was to an artisan in a vision ; the second to a Priest, who was walking into the country ; the third revelation was made to a *religieuse* at Naples, who, whilst one day prostrating herself before a little statue of St. Philomene, had her eyes forcibly shut against her will, so that no efforts of hers could open them, whilst a sweet voice addressed her thus : ' My dear sister, I am the daughter of a Prince in Greece ; my father and mother were idolaters, and a long time without children ; but a Physician promised them posterity if they would be baptized ; they did so ; in consequence I was born. Some business led my family to Rome, when Diocletian fell in love with me ; but I had made a promise two years before to Jesus Christ, and would not break my promise. Neither the threats nor caresses of Diocletian had any effect upon me. Finding me invincible, he ordered that I should be thrown into the Tiber with an anchor round my neck ; but as it was about to be executed, two angels appeared, and cut the rope, so that the anchor fell into the Tiber, and they carried me away. But Diocletian ordered his archers to shoot me ; but the arrows refused to second their attempt. He then ordered the darts to be made red hot, and directed against me a second time ; but the darts having traversed a part of the distance towards me, took all at once a contrary direction, and struck those who had thrown them. At length the tyrant cut off my head, and I was received into heaven.'

429.

0

C. Richards, Printer, 100, St. Martin's-lane, Charing Cross.

5

" In 1805 Don Francis went to Rome, and wanting a holy body for his domestic chapel, went to a room where the sacred relics are deposited. In coming into the presence of Philomene's bones, he was seized with a sudden and extraordinary joy, which led him to ask for her bones. After some difficulty, they were given to him ; and were deposited in a chest inside the carriage, on the outside of which the Bishop and Don Francis sat. But they had scarcely got out of town, when the Bishop perceived himself struck forcibly over the legs, and complained to the driver of the bad arrangement of the packages. The Bishop resumed his seat, but the blows became more violent than ever : in consequence, the chest was put into the fore-part of the carriage ; when instantly the prodigy ceased, and the Bishop and his attendants begged pardon of the saint for not putting her bones in the most honourable part of the carriage."

It is to be hoped that Popish Priests will in future be more careful in what manner they stow away their relics when travelling. The shins of the Bishop were justly battered for his unintentional want of respect for his betters. There is no telling what might be the punishment of a refractory omnibus driver, or an heretical cabman, on a similar occasion. These Popish saints, especially female ones, are capricious and ticklish beings, as will appear in the sequel of the volume. This lady performs all kinds of miracles, cures every disease incident to the human frame, raises the dead, prolongs the life of the living ; and actually does every thing that all the quack medicines have ever promised to do.

Don Francis very soon finds he has more on his hands than he bargained for. The lady waxes wroth, and one night tears up her old clothes, and insists on having a new suit; which being supplied, she becomes peaceable. Her hair is bald upon one part of her head, but grows most beautifully in a few hours, without any application of Macassar oil, or anything beyond the prayers of the faithful. By and by she " sweats ; two streams run down her face, which unite at her chin, and descend in a

429.

thin thread to her breast: this melts the hearts of the obstinate, and converts them." By some means or other she gets into a ditch. Here she rescues a child who tumbles in ; the child, however, has fortunately a piece of paper in its pocket that belongs to the saint herself, and acts as a passport through the mud and dirt in the trench.—This is the sort of stuff which on the Continent, where the doctrines and discipline of Popery are in their full vigour, has superseded the use of the holy Scriptures ; and the kind of commodity which in religious instruction, to the poor of this country and Ireland, the priesthood of Antichrist would willingly substitute for the Bible. The Bishop of Geneva has given his authority for the publication of this volume, and has added, " He thinks, according to the example of his colleagues in the Popish Episcopacy, to further the designs of divine Providence by recommending to all his Diocesans devotion to St. Philomene."

Leo XII. blessed the saint. The present Pope Gregory XVI. blessed one of her images destined to receive public worship in the capital of the Popish world. In the last chapter is this form of prayer: " O faithful virgin and glorious martyr, have pity on me ; exercise both on my soul and body the office or ministry of salvation, of which God hath judged you worthy, better than I do. You know the multitude and diversity of my wants : behold me at your feet full of misery and of hope. I solicit your charity : O great saint, hear me favourably ; bless me ; vouchsafe to make acceptable to my God the humble supplication which I present to you."

One of the most absurd and anti-scriptural doctrines of Popery is that of " indulgences." According to this dogma, all the good works of the saints, over and above those which are necessary towards their own salvation, are deposited together with the merits of Jesus Christ in one inexhaustible treasury. The keys of this, it is said, were committed to St. Peter, and to his successors the Popes, who may open it at pleasure, and by transferring

429.

C. Richards, Printer, 100, St. Martin's-lane, Charing Cross.

a portion of this superabundant merit to any particular person, for a sum of money, may convey to him either the pardon of his own sins, or a release for any for whom he is interested, from the pains of purgatory. Such indulgences were first invented in the eleventh century by Urban II., as a recompence for those who went in person upon the perilous enterprise of conquering the Holy Land. Pope Leo X., in order to carry on the magnificent structure of St. Peter's at Rome, published indulgences, and a plenary remission to all such as should contribute money towards it. Finding the project take, he granted to Albert, Elector of Mentz, the benefit of the indulgences of Saxony, and the neighbouring parts; and farmed out those of other countries to the highest bidders; who, to make the best of their bargain, procured the ablest Preachers to cry up the value of their ware. A part of the form of these indulgences was as follows :—" I remit to you all punishment which you deserve in purgatory; and I restore you to the holy sacraments of the Church, to the unity of the faithful, and to that innocence and purity which you possessed at baptism; so that when you die, the gates of punishment shall be shut, and the gates of the paradise of delight shall be opened; and if you should not die at present, this grace shall remain in full force when you are at the point of death. In the name of the Father, and of the Son, and of the Holy Ghost." Hence a book is published which contains the exact sum to be levied for the pardon of each particular sin; such as, " Taking a false oath, 9s.; for burning a neighbour's house, 12s.; for robbing, 12s.; for murdering a layman, 7s.; for laying violent hands on a Clergyman, 10s. 6d." Various other sins are mentioned, some of which are of such an' indelicate nature, that I will not defile my paper by mentioning them, nor make my readers blush while reading them. The terms in which the retailers of indulgences described their benefits, and the necessity of purchasing them, were so extravagant, that they appear almost incredible. "If any man," said they, "purchase

429.

letters of indulgence, his soul may rest secure with respect to his salvation. The souls confined in purgatory, for whose redemption indulgences are purchased, as soon as the money tinkles in the chest, instantly escape from that place of torment, and ascend into heaven. That the efficacy of indulgences is so great, that the most heinous sins, even if one should violate (which is impossible) the mother of God, would be remitted and expiated by them, and the person be freed both from punishment and guilt. This is the unspeakable gift of God to reconcile men to himself." " Lo," said they, " the heavens are opened: if you enter not now, when will you enter? For twelve-pence you may redeem the soul of your father from purgatory. And are you so ungrateful that you will not rescue the soul of your parent from torment? If you had but one coat, you ought to strip yourself instantly, and sell it in order to purchase such a benefit." During the reign of Queen Elizabeth, the Pope excited Sir Thomas Stuckley to raise a rebellion in Ireland. Stuckley engaged to conquer that kingdom for the Pope ; and the holy father furnished him with a number of crucifixes, by selling of which he was to make his own fortune. The following are among the number of indulgences granted to these crucifixes :—" Whoso beholdeth with reverence and devotion one of these crosses, as oft as he doth it, getteth fifty days of indulgence."—"And for the increase and exaltation of the holy Catholic faith, and for the extirpation of heretics, he shall have fifty days of indulgence, and upon festival-days one hundred."—" In going to any conflict or feat of arms against the enemies of our holy faith, he shall obtain seven years of indulgence."— " As oft as he shall be confessed and *houseled*, making his prayers by word or mind, before the most holy crucifix, and praying for the prosperous state of the holy Church, and for the chief Bishop, and for the reducing of the realms of England and Scotland, he shall obtain all the indulgences that are granted for visiting all the holy places that are both within and

429.

C. Richards, Printer, 100, St. Martin's-lane, Charing Cross.

without the gates of Rome."—" Whoso shall use 'and accustom to behold it with devotion to the cross, saying five paternosters, five aves, and some other prayers to our Saviour, or our Lady, &c., he shall obtain once in his life full indulgence of all his sins, besides the other indulgence of fifty days for each time that he prayeth." —" That every Friday that mass is said, or caused to be said, upon any altar where one of these crucifixes is set, one soul shall be released out of purgatory."

Such are some, of the figments of Popery; such the impositions that are practised on the ignorant and the credulous. But what man in his sober senses, with the Scriptures in his hands, can imagine that these things form any part of Christianity? Where is purgatory taught in the Bible? Where are we instructed to believe, that there is in the world of spirits an intermediate state midway between heaven and hell ; and that some are too bad for the former, and too good for the latter? The New Testament teaches us, that at death, " he that is filthy shall be filthy still," and " he that is righteous shall be righteous still." But even supposing that there was such a place as purgatory, and that unholy souls were sent there to be purified from sin, what a monstrous absurdity that the possession of a little crucifix, or the offering of a few shillings to the Priest, could avail to rescue souls from the punishment they are justly doomed to suffer! And if money can procure the release of souls from purgatory, it can of course prevent them from going there ; and the marvel is, that Papists should not compromise matters with their Priests, and pay down in their lifetime a few shillings, that when they die they may pass to paradise, without suffering the pains of purgatory. And if the Pope's indulgences can release souls from purgatory, why does he not at once release them all? Where is his love for the souls of his flock? To keep men in torment, until money is paid for their release, is to make merchandise of them? And why does not the Pope keep himself out of purgatory? For the many masses offered for him after his death, which are never intended for those in heaven or hell, proclaim that he himself, in the estimation of the Priests, is gone to the flames of purgatory. But, alas, "the god of this world hath blinded the minds of them that believe not." And men more completely blinded by the devil, and his agents the Priests, than Papists, are not to be found upon the earth. We pity Pagans, we marvel at their ignorance, and are surprised at their superstitions, and the method to which they resort for propitiating their idol-gods. But there is nothing in all the annals of Paganism more ridiculous and absurd than many of the practices of Papists. Let the reader peruse the following account, and then judge for himself :—

In the county of Down in Ireland, there are some celebrated wells of St. Patrick ; and every Midsummer's-eve thousands of Roman Catholics, many from distant parts of the country, resort to these holy wells to cleanse their souls from sin, and clear their mortal bodies of diseases. The influx of people of different ranks for some nights before the one in which alone these wells possess this power, (for on all other days and nights in the year they rank not above common draw-wells,) is prodigious ; and their attendants, hordes of beggars, whose ragged garments if once taken off could not be put on again by the ingenuity of man, infest the streets and lanes, and choose their lodgings in the highways and hedges. "Having," says the writer, "been previously informed of the approach of this miraculous night, and having made ourselves acquainted with the locality of the wells, early in the evening we repaired to the spot. We had been told that we should see something quite new to us ; and we met with what was scarcely credible on ocular evidence. The spot on which this scene of superstitious folly was exhibited, was admirably adapted to heighten every attendant circumstance of it ; the wonderful wells, of which there are four, being situated in a square or patch of ground surrounded by steep rocks, which reverberated every sound, and redoubled all the confusion. The *coup d'œil* of the square, on our approach, presented a
429.

C. Richards, Printer, 100, St. Martin's-lane, Charing Cross.

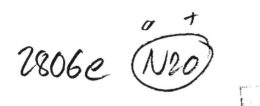

11

floating mass of various-coloured heads; and our ears
were astonished with confused and mingled sounds of
mirth and sorrow, of frantic enthusiastic joy, and deep
desponding ravings. On descending into the square,
we found ourselves immediately in the midst of innu-
merable groups of these fanatics, running in all direc-
tions, confusedly in appearance, but methodically as we
afterwards found in reality. The men and women were
barefooted; and the heads of all were bound round with
handkerchiefs. Some were running in circles, some
kneeling in groups, some were singing in wild concert,
some were jumping about like maniacs, at the end of an
old building, which we were told was the ruins of a chapel
erected, with several adjacent buildings, in one miraculous
Midsummer's night by the tutelar saint of the wells; of
whose talent as a mason they give, it must be confessed,
no very exalted opinion. When we had somewhat
recovered from the first surprise, which the unaccountably
fantastic actions of the crowd had given us, we endea-
voured to trace the progress of some of these deluded
votaries through all the mazes of their mystic penance.
The first object of them all appeared to be, the ascent of
the steepest and most rugged part of the rock, up which
both men and women crawled their painful way on their
hands and bare knees. The men's clothes were all
made so as to accommodate their knees with all the
sharpness of the pointed rock; and the poor women,
many of them young and beautiful, took incredible
pains to prevent their petticoats from affording any
defence against these torturing asperities. Covered with
dust and perspiration and blood, they at last reached
the summit of the rock, where in a rude sort of chair,
hewn out of the stone, sat an old man, who seemed to
be the High Priest of this religious frenzy. In his hat
each of the penitents deposited a halfpenny; after which,
he turned them round a certain number of times, lis-
tened to the long catalogue of their offences, and
dictated to them the penance they were to undergo or
perform. They then descended the rock by another
429.

path, but in the same manner and posture, equally
careful to be cut by the flints, and to suffer as much as
possible. This was perhaps more painful travelling than
the ascent had been: the suffering knees were rubbed
another way; every step threatened a tumble; and if
any thing could have been lively there, the ridiculous
attitudes of these descenders, would have made us so.
When they gained the foot of the hill, they most of
them bestowed a small donation of charity on some
miserable groups of supplicants, who were stationed
there. One beggar, a cripple, sat on the ground, at one
moment addressing the crowd behind him, and swearing
that all the Protestants ought to be burnt out of the
country; and in the same breath begging the penitents
to give him one halfpenny, for the love of 'swate
blessed Jasus.' The penitents now returned to the use
of their feet, and commenced a running sort of Irish-
jiggish walk, round several cairns, or heaps of stones,
erected at different spaces: this lasted for some time.
Suddenly they would prostrate themselves before the
cairn, and ejaculate some hasty prayers; and as
suddenly rise, and resume their mill-horse circumrota-
tion. Their eyes were fixed; their looks spoke anxiety,
almost despair; and the operations of their faculties
seemed totally suspended. They then proceeded to one
end of the old chapel, and seemed to believe that there
was a virtue unknown to us heretics in *one particular
stone* of the building, which every one was careful to
touch with the right hand: those who were tall did it
easily; those who were short, left no mode of jumping
unpractised to accomplish it. But the most remarkable
and, doubtless, the most efficient of the ceremonies, was
reserved for the last; and surely nothing that was ever
devised by man, more forcibly evinced how low our
nature can descend. Around the largest of the wells,
which was in a building, very much, to common eyes,
like a stable, all those who had performed their penances
were assembled; some dressing, some undressing, *many
stark naked.* A certain number of them were admitted
429.

C. Richards, Printer, 100, St. Martin's-lane, Charing Cross.

at a time into this *holy* well; and there, men and
women of every age bathed promiscuously, without any
covering. They undressed before bathing, and performed
the whole business of the toilet afterwards, in the open air,
in the midst of the crowd, without appearing sensible of
the observations of the lookers-on, perfectly regardless
of decency, and perfectly dead to all natural sensations.
The penance having terminated, the penitents adjourned
either to booths or tents, to drink, or join their friends.
The air then rang with musical monotonous singing,
which became louder with every glass of whisky;
finishing in frolicsome debauch, and laying, in all
probability, the foundation for future penances, and
more thorough ablutions. No pen can describe all the
confusion; no description can give a just idea of the
noise and disorder which filled this *hallowed* square,
this theatre of fanaticism, this temple of superstition.
The minor parts of the spectacle were filled up with
credulous mothers, half-drowning their poor children to
cure their sore eyes; with cripples who exhibited every
thing that has yet been discovered in deformity, ex-
pecting to be washed straight, and to walk away nimble
and comely; and though nobody was cured, nobody
went away doubting. Shouting, and howling, and
swearing, and carousings, filled up every pause, and
threw over this spot the air of earth and hell. I was
never more shocked and struck with horror. I perceived
many of them intoxicated with religious fervour and
all-potent whisky, and warming into violence before
midnight, at which time the distraction was at its climax."

Such are the genuine fruits of Popery; and such the
debasement, superstition, and degradation to which it
leads. What is there in Paganism more absurd or
preposterous than the adoration of holy wells, moth-
eaten vestments, or rotten bones? And how deeply to
be deplored, that men should be taught that this is
religion; that this forms a part of their duty to God!
And what can equal the guilt of those who take away
the key of knowledge; who enter not into the kingdom
429.

of God themselves, and those who would enter they hinder? That many Romish Priests know better, can scarcely be doubted. They are men of learning and science, and they have access to numerous treatises on theology; but alas! "by this craft" they have their "wealth;" and one of the distinctive marks of the last days is, that "men shall be lovers of themselves." And what profound lovers of themselves Popish Priests are, the following facts sufficiently illustrate :—

In Ireland there are what are called "Stations for Confessing." It was formerly the custom, at whatever house these stations were held, to require that a dinner be provided for the Priest: and as the host would not set down the Priest by himself, it was always the practice to invite fifteen or twenty of the neighbouring farmers, and their wives, who were 'expected to attend at confession, and who would ask them in return. "And I have frequently seen," says the writer, "purchased for these occasions, meat, several gallons of whisky, &c., and always a *bottle of wine for the Priest's own drinking*. This was not all: there was a tax of five shillings on the landlord for saying the mass, who was made to believe that a temporal and spiritual blessing would follow. Besides this, it was expected that each confessed person would pay something for absolution. For causes best known to themselves, these dinner-parties were, of late years, changed for breakfasts, which were more couvenient for the Priest, as he had to return home, when these stations were held in the country, some miles, and he might not so clearly see his way. As the Priest is seldom ready before twelve o'clock, these breakfasts usually commence about that time. The bill of fare is as follows:—tea, a hot griddle-cake, butter, eggs, &c., &c., with *decanters of whisky* placed on the breakfast-table; and as the Irish have a great affection for the *native*, as they call whisky, these decanters are frequently replenished, and the feast prolonged for the remainder of the day. The writer was present at the settlement of an account with the spirit-dealer, for the
429

C. Richards, Printer, 100, St. Martin's-lane, Charing Cross.

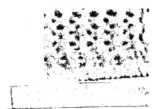

whisky drank at but *one* breakfast-station for confession, at his opposite neighbour's house, where the whole company, men, women, and children, could not have exceeded twenty-four persons; when the bill, admitted to be correct, and paid for, was seven half-gallons of whisky, at sixteen shillings per gallon,—a liquor considerably stronger than either brandy or rum. It is the practice of the Priest to publish from the altar, at certain periods of the year, that he will hold stations for confession, at certain houses, then and there named. These houses are selected, without previous liberty obtained from the owners, perhaps, lest they should make objections; which many of them would most certainly do, if not thus publicly given out from the altar."

The Papists believe, according to Mr. Gavin, that "purgatory is divided into eight apartments; that the lowest of these is occupied by the souls of poor persons, and the highest, by the souls of Kings; and that the degree of torment which the souls in purgatory suffer, is in proportion to the dignity of the apartments which they occupy; those in the lower vaults suffering less, and those in the higher ones suffering more, for no other reason than that the friends of the latter are supposed able to pay large sums for relief, while the friends of the former can pay little or nothing; and it must be allowed to be equitable, at least in Popish reckoning, that if the rich heirs of Kings and Princes do not pay liberally for the repose of the souls of their deceased friends, the deceased must pay the debt of suffering in their own persons; whereas the poor souls whose friends have little to pay, will get off after suffering a little.

" This arrangement is admirably calculated to enrich the dealers in masses, which are understood to have such efficacy in procuring relief to the souls in purgatory. The more wicked they had been, the better for the Church, provided they left plenty of money, as the more masses were necessary for their relief; and the price of masses is understood to bear some proportion to the wealth of the person at whose request, and on whose behalf, they are said. If a Priest or a man has only dreamed that such a one's father or mother is suffering dreadful torments in purgatory, this will be enough to command a thousand masses, and a thousand guineas to pay for them, if the relations of the deceased be able to pay so much : if not, the Priests will take what they can give for the present, and more when they can get it."

Thus it may be seen how much the moral principle is degraded by such a system, and even by the Priests; a system that holds out to its deluded followers a yearly or half-yearly acquittal for sin. Well may that truth, applied by our Saviour to the Scribes and Pharisees, be applied to them : " Ye compass sea and land to gain one proselyte ; and when ye have gained him, ye make him twofold more a child of the devil."

Price 5s. 4d. per 100. Considerable allowance will be made to Tract-Societies, Sunday-Schools, and Booksellers.

London: R. Needham, Printer, 1, Belle-Sauvage-Yard, Ludgate-Hill.
429

C. Richards, Printer, 100, St. Martin's-lane, Charing Cross.

CPSIA information can be obtained
at www.ICGtesting.com
Printed in the USA
BVHW090317211118
533509BV00032BA/5004/P